SHARING
THE
SALT

Ida Glaser & Shaylesh Raja

SCRIPTURE UNION

Scripture Union, 207–209 Queensway, Bletchley, MK2 2EB, England.

First published 1999, reprinted 1999

ISBN 1 85999 307 9

British Library Cataloguing-in-Publication Data
A catalogue record for this book is available from the British Library.

Cover design by David Lund.

Printed and bound in Great Britain by Cox & Wyman, Reading, Berkshire.

CONTENTS

FOREWORD

Pamela was still only a young woman, but already she had had a husband who was a pimp, been divorced, started another long-term relationship, suffered several miscarriages, been raped and then got caught up in prostitution as well as Hari Krishna. She was desperate and, in her words, 'about to take the tablets to end it all'. How could God help someone like her?

The answer was surprisingly simple – through friendship. A girl who sometimes looked after Pamela's children (yes, she had those too!) invited her to a coffee bar at the church across the road. There she met a 'middle-class woman' who, much to her surprise, had a similar story to Pamela's. In a few weeks, this woman was able to assure Pamela of acceptance and support not only from herself but also from Jesus. Pamela found this friendship to be real and, although she still has a lot to sort out, she is gradually making it! Such is the gospel power in Christian friendship.

This series, 'Relating Good News', is intended to help us maximise the opportunities for evangelism in our relationships and to become more relational people. Today, quality relationships have proved to be the most effective way of winning people to Christ. Jesus himself understood the value of good relationships for his ministry, as did Paul – someone who knew well how important it was to 'become all things to all people so that some may believe'. We too must recognise that, in an age when 'the medium is the message', the quality of our relationships will greatly affect our ability to communicate an adequate gospel.

Not all our friendships will be intense and long-lasting (think of the babysitter's role in Pamela's life), yet we can learn how to make the most of the brief encounters too. The books in this series, therefore, are about equipping us to be effective in sharing God's good news within the whole variety of relationships we may have. If you want to be better at relating, if you long to see your relationships honour Christ, if you desire to see the people you know become friends of Christ, my prayer is that you will find here all you need to help you as you seek to share your faith as well as your friendship.

David Spriggs
Consulting Editor

Shaylesh Raja
and Ida Glaser

invite you to

Sharing the Salt

Date: Today

Time: Whenever you like

Place: Your most comfortable
chair

'WELCOME!'

'Hello, I'm **Shaylesh**! Having spent much of my early adolescence virtually living in a Hindu temple, you might think I would know God well. But I found that, no matter how hard I tried, God was always just out of reach. I remember praying, "God, if you are there, show yourself to me." I had to wait nearly ten years to have that prayer answered – when I turned to Jesus. Then I discovered that I could meet with God in a way I had never imagined. When I pray, I know God hears – and he answers!

'At first I wanted to go and tell people in India about Jesus, but then I was led to look at the growing numbers of my community in UK. They need to hear too. So many are searching for God, but it is only through Jesus that they will know him. No other faith promises that personal relationship with the Creator.

'I am married with four children and live in Leicester. Here we have many opportunities to befriend people of many cultures and faith; may we always use these opportunities wisely!'

'I'm **Ida**. I'm half Czech Jew and half English Gentile, and have been aiming to share the love of Jesus with Muslim people since God called me in that direction when I was twenty. Since then I've done all sorts of things, including four years' teaching Physics to Muslim girls overseas and seven years working with a local church project in inner city Newcastle upon Tyne. I've visited Asian homes, run a children's club in my home, been part of a community coping with crime and racism, and helped Christian people to reach out to their Asian neighbours. I've realised that the best place to start is to make friends across all the barriers of race, class, culture, age and religion, which so often separate human beings from each other – even the Jewish-Muslim barrier. Crossing the barriers is what God was doing when he sent Jesus!'

Ours is a cross-cultural friendship. We started as acquaintances, then decided that we could work as a well-mixed team – brown and white, eastern and western, male and female, Jew and Gentile, experiencing Asian faiths as an insider and as an outsider, knowing about Hinduism and knowing about Islam. As we have worked together, we have become friends. We have had to learn patience with each other, to understand each other's points of view and appreciate each other's contributions. Neither of us could have produced this book alone, but together…? Well, we'll leave you to judge.

This book is not an instruction manual, full of 'dos' and 'don'ts'. Instead, it simply shares many real-life experiences and invites you to learn from them. You might like to try acting out some of the stories with a friend or a group from your church. That way, you can get 'inside' the story and begin to feel the issues as well as to think about your own friendships. We also offer help from the Bible, along with some 'things to think about' – you might find it worthwhile discussing these with a friend or a group. We do not offer answers to these because there aren't any right answers. Every friendship is unique with its own peculiar joys and trials.

So come and join us as we think about our friendships

with Sikhs, Hindus and Muslims! We invite you to pray for those you may come into contact with as you read this book. We will be praying that God will help you to establish strong and long-lasting relationships with them.

WHY 'SHARING THE SALT?

Eating together is at the heart of friendship in many cultures. Relationships are sealed as we visit each other's homes and share what God has given to us. But hospitality is not only an important part of Asian cultures: it was also very important in Bible times. Jesus often went to eat with people, and following him is sometimes described in terms of eating together. He invites us to join his heavenly banquet (Matt 22:1–10; 26:26–29) and promises to come and eat with us if we will let him (Rev 3:20). 'Sharing salt' is a picture of God's friendship to us as well as our friendships with others.

Welcome!
Khush Amdeed!

स्वागतम्

આવો પધારો

ਜੀ ਆਇਆਂ ਨੂੰ

स्वागत

خوش آمدید

INTRODUCTION

We had been friends for six years. Now we were going together to visit her cousins in another town. 'What does it mean that you are a missionary?' she asked. And then, as I explained, she asked, 'If I don't become a Christian, will you still be my friend?'

Her question has remained with me through all my relationships with non-Christian people. Why am I relating to them? Will I stay with them? What would Jesus do? And I have asked myself, 'What does it really mean to be a friend?'

I go back to a little book given to me by the same Muslim friend – lovingly chosen from a Christian bookshop. On the front is written:

A FRIEND is one who
KNOWS you as you are,
UNDERSTANDS where you've been,
ACCEPTS who you've become,
and still gently INVITES you to grow.
Thank you for being my friend.

Friendship and evangelism are not necessarily the same. A friend is not someone who is always trying to preach at you. A friend is someone who relates to you as a person, someone you feel 'at home' with, someone you can rely on.

Yet, for a Christian, being a friend *is* sharing the gospel.

The gospel teaches us who we are
… that we are precious beings, made in the image of God, created to relate to him and to each other. If we treat our friends like that, we will be relating this good news.

The gospel teaches us that we are fallen, but God still loves us
If we see our friends with all their faults, see ourselves with all our faults, and yet we still love them, we will be relating this good news.

The gospel breaks down all barriers
… between human beings and God, and between different kinds of human beings. If we can be friends across cultural and religious barriers, we will be relating this good news.

The gospel teaches us that God is concerned with our deepest joys and hurts
If we can share our friends' concerns and help them to share them with our Lord, we will be relating this good news.

If our relationships are real friendships, we will be able to share the things that most matter to us. We will be able to talk about our longings, our beliefs and our deepest loves. We will even be able to speak about God.

Talking about God is often much easier when we are with friends who are religious than with friends who have no religion at all. Christians may sometimes wonder whether their Western friends live in a different world or speak a different language, the idea of God seems so alien to them. With Muslims and Hindus and Sikhs it is different. They live in a world where God matters. They may believe different things about him, but they know he is there and that their lives depend on him. So they find it natural to talk about him, and about what he wants from them. They are often delighted to explain what their faith means to them.

This means that, as Christians, we can speak of what the Lord Jesus means to us. We can draw on the Bible as we share our problems with them. We may even find that we can invite them to celebrate with us, to meet other Christians and hear more about Jesus.

Real friendship always enriches, but making friends with someone from a different culture or with different beliefs gives us the unique opportunity to learn all sorts of new things. Some of these discoveries will challenge us, some will puzzle us, some will give us great pleasure, and some will make us sad. All will offer us the chance to learn more about ourselves and to grow closer to God. Growing friendships may present problems, prompt questions and even demand sacrifices. But they bring lots of fun with them too!

WHY BOTHER?

Perhaps you have plenty of friends. Perhaps you have as much fun as you want. Perhaps you feel you could do without the sacrifices and the demands of forming a friendship with a Hindu, a Sikh or a Muslim.

We could give all sorts of reasons why you should bother. It will be good for you. It will build good community relations in your area. It will give you opportunities for evangelism. It will give you the opportunity to eat real curry whenever you want! However, here is the most important reason: *it will please the Lord Jesus Christ, who calls us to love our neighbours*.

The original commandment, 'Love your neighbour as yourself', comes in Leviticus 19 – twice. The first time, it refers to neighbours who are the same as we are:

> Do not hate your brother in your heart. Rebuke
> your neighbour frankly so that you will not
> share in his guilt.
>   Do not seek revenge or bear a grudge against

one of your people, but love your neighbour as
yourself. I am the Lord. *(vs 17–18)*

The second time, it refers to those who are different:

When an alien lives with you in your land, do
not ill-treat him. The alien living with you must
be treated as one of your native-born. Love him
as yourself, for you were aliens in Egypt. I am
the Lord your God. *(vs 33–34)*

The 'alien' is singled out as one needing special love.

We are to love others

- because the Lord is our God. If we belong to the Lord, we
  should love those whom he loves – and that means
  everyone.

- because we share some of their experience. If we follow
  Jesus, we will have at least the experience of thinking
  differently from the people around us.

Jesus' explanation of this law was the parable of the Good
Samaritan (Luke 10:25–37). He overturned the racial preju-
dice of his day by making the member of the despised ethnic
minority the hero of the story. We are to 'go and do likewise'. One way of 'doing likewise' is to make friends.

BEFORE YOU GO ANY FURTHER

Can we invite you to pray? Pray for yourself, for your
church, for any Hindus, Sikhs or Muslims you may know,
for the community you live in, for the friends God is going
to give you.

In this book, we will be looking at very human questions.
Relating across cultures is challenging, and we all need help
to do it. But there is another dimension…

We are not fighting against flesh and blood

In fact, we want to put an end to the 'fighting' mentality. Too many of us see people of different religions as somehow our enemies. All of us have some prejudices about people of different races and cultures. We pray that this book will help Christians to see their own prejudices, to repent of them and have them replaced by the grace and love of God.

We are fighting against the spiritual forces of evil in the heavenly places

The forces of evil do not like Christians to relate to people of other religions. They do not like to see love growing between people of different cultures, because this is a sign of God's love. They hate it when people come to Christ.

So do not be surprised if you are discouraged at times or tempted to give up. Keep praying, keep trusting, and eventually you will find great joy, both in your friendships and in relating the Good News.

Chapter 1

FRIENDSHIP, EAST AND WEST

WHAT IS A FRIEND?

I can still remember the beginning of my friendship with Barbara. Yes, I had friends already. I had people to talk to, people who would visit my home, people to 'hang around' with at school ... but this was different. We had gone to visit Barbara's aunt, and had decided to escape the adults for a walk across the hill. Suddenly we were talking about our feelings – about life, about others, about God – and I knew that here was someone who cared about the things I cared about, someone who would be very special to me. The wonder was that she felt the same – we would be friends. More than thirty years later, separated by thousands of miles, and having gone in very different directions in life, we are still friends. We write seldom and meet less, but the old rapport is still there. This is a relationship that matters.

Who is your friend? What does he or she mean to you? What has it cost you to retain that friendship?

To think about

According to the Chambers Twentieth Century Dictionary, a friend is 'one loving or attached to another; an intimate acquaintance; a favourer, well-wisher'. But friendship means different things to different people.

- Think about the friendships that are important to you. Then write down three things you want to thank God for in each of those friends.

- How have these friendships helped you to get to know the Lord Jesus Christ?

Shaylesh thinks about what friendship means to him. He observes different levels of friendship:

Acquaintances

'Our local Asian shopkeeper knows me. He is polite and welcoming. Yes, he wants my custom, but he has also taken a personal interest in me and my family. When my children come to the shop with me, he chats with them. We always have something to talk about apart from shopping. We converse about life and current affairs. We can laugh together. We can say to mutual acquaintances, "Yes, I know him." He knows my shopping habits, like a pub landlord knows the usual and is ready pouring it as soon as a regular customer walks in.

'A work colleague is another acquaintance. We work together well and have a lot in common regarding business matters. We are from the same ethnic background, so we have an extra common bond. We have daily dealings with each other and have often worked as a team. He knows my strengths and weaknesses, and I know his. We are also able to converse about faith.'

A friend

'He is all that an acquaintance is, with added value. I can trust my friend enough to ask him favours of a personal nature.

'I once helped out as a volunteer at an Asian lunch club in a community centre. The volunteers served the lunches, cleaned up after them, and then had lunch together. Over two years, I got to know one of the volunteers well, especially when we began to serve on the club's management committee together. I visited my new friend at his home, and got to know his disabled wife, who was a member of the lunch club. We built up trust, so that one day he asked if I could give him a personal reference relating to a legal matter he was conducting on behalf of his wife. A friend is someone with whom you can share a personal need.'

A good friend

'She is a family friend. All the family like her to drop in. She can relate to the children as well as to the adults. She is fun-loving, and the children often ask about her. "We haven't seen Auntie for a long time," they complain.

'She is trustworthy and can keep a confidence. The Asian community is close and prone to gossip of every nature. A good friend will not go around spreading gossip in the community. She will not dishonour the family name by breaking confidence. She will help in every way she can. Given time, she will be known as one of the family.'

One of the family

'"One of us" is how a real friend is introduced to family and friends. He or she is not called "friend", but "brother" or "sister" or "grandmother" or "grandfather".'

Mary was the co-ordinator of her local mother's union. She made friends with her Asian neighbour, Shantaben. Shantaben was a grandmother and a widow like Mary. She had very little English, and Mary did not a speak a word of Gujerati, Shantaben's mother tongue.

Mary tried to communicate in broken English and Shantaben tried to respond as much as she could. They often got muddled, talking at cross purposes and misunderstanding each other. Sometimes they laughed, and sometimes they got frustrated, but they liked each other so they kept trying. Mary prayed for Shantaben and became a friend of the family. Shantaben's son, daughter, grandchildren, son-in-law, daughter-in-law all liked Mary. Soon the grandchildren began to call Mary 'Grandma'.

Mary felt very privileged! She took her new role very seriously. She began to learn about the important things that shaped her new family. She found out about the special dates and times in their lives. She looked up their important festivals, and sat with Shantaben and her daughter, trying to understand what the festivals meant to them. How do they help them to worship God? What do the events leading up to the festival mean? What is the background to a particular festival? What does Shantaben do at the temple? In what ways does she feel that God is close to her? What about assurance of eternal life? All these Mary began to ponder, understand, and appreciate.

Mary was accepted and respected as one of the elders of the family.

'Being part of a family brings responsibilities. Asian families ask favours, which at times may be hard work.'

An Asian family adopted John, a single student, as son and brother. A need arose for a trip to the airport to collect grandpa arriving from India. They did not own a car, but John did. John was asked a couple of days before if he could drive them to the airport for 7 am. They assumed that he would help: after all, he was part of the family. Unfortunately, it clashed with John's early morning tutorial. John had learnt Asian ways and, as much as he could, tried to help them to respect his culture and his ways. He saw the importance of this request and swapped his tutorial so that he could help.

'However, there may also be sacrificial giving on the part of the Asian family.'

Shantaben's daughter moved town. It was two hours on the coach to get to her new home. The children wanted so much to see Grandma Mary that they insisted that she be invited to stay with them for a week. Mary did not know what to do. She was fearful that she might offend them in some way by her behaviour. Would she be able to read her Bible? Would she be able to eat the hot curried food? She was unsure how they would cope with her.

Eventually, Mary decided to go. She really wanted to see her adopted daughter and grandchildren. On the way to their new home from the bus station, the first thing she was shown was the church, which she could attend on Sunday morning. Mary was shown her own room where she could read her Bible in peace and quietness. The meals were mainly English. In the evenings Mary was asked to read some stories from the Bible.

Mary was touched. She knew what it had cost her new family to make her feel so 'at home'. They were Hindus and strict vegetarians – they did not even eat eggs. To have meat in their home made it unclean, spiritually. To store that meat in their freezer made the other food in it unclean and fit only to be thrown away. To cook and eat meat in the usual household utensils would make them unclean, however much they were washed afterwards. The family had loved their Grandma Mary enough to break some of their rules for her. She had wondered whether she would be able to cope with visiting them. Now she wondered how they had been able to cope with her visit!

WHAT'S THE DIFFERENCE?

Most cultures have ideas of what is an acquaintance, a friend, a good friend, 'one of us'. But there are differences.

THINK ABOUT PEOPLE YOU KNOW
- An acquaintance

- A friend
- A good friend
- Someone who really belongs, who is one of us

Read again what Shaylesh says above about different sorts of friendships, then fill in the table opposite:

Some differences will be the result of personality, but some are probably because of culture. If you think like a Westerner, you may have noticed that Easterners have different expectations of friendship.

There are also similarities: for example, friends East and West expect to trust each other. At the acquaintance stage, both look for some sort of common ground – a place to meet, a common interest. As the friendship grows, both Easterners and Westerners become more able to share personal matters and to ask each other for help.

Perhaps the biggest difference is the place of the *family*. While most Westerners think of themselves as individuals first and members of families second, most Easterners living in Britain still think of themselves first as members of a family. This means that any close friendship will involve relating with a family. This in turn will mean *hospitality*. Offering hospitality, and especially food, is an important part of Eastern cultures. A visitor to an Asian home seldom leaves without being fed. A guest is always offered refreshment, and a host will be very disappointed if it is refused. He or she may even be offended. Guests often come a long way to make a visit and may stay for several days. This is not seen as an inconvenience: it is a great privilege for the host to honour his guests by providing food and shelter. He will give them the best he can provide, at whatever cost, and feel that he has been honoured by their visit. Eating together – 'sharing salt' – honours visitors and hosts alike. It is at such times that friendships are bonded, deals are closed and settled disputes are celebrated.

	Shaylesh's friend	My friend	Mary's friend, Shantaben	My very close friend
Things in common	Age, culture, gender, lunch club		Age, gender, grandmothers	
Differences	Religion		Culture, religion, language	
What they do together	Work, talk		Talk, visit, share lives	
Relationship with friend's family				
The cost of friendship				
The gains of friendship				

Travelling through Afghanistan, Tom's jeep broke down. It was late at night, and he stopped in a small village. There were no hotels or inns, so he knocked on the first door he found, wondering what would happen.

The owner of the house had no English, and Tom had no Kurdish. Using sign language, he managed to communicate that he needed somewhere to sleep. The owner gave Tom a floor space and some blankets. It was pitch dark, and Tom was quickly asleep. Some time later, the owner woke him with a bowl of soup in his hands. It smelt wonderful, and the warmth and spice ensured that Tom slept like a log for the rest of the night.

In the morning, people came to welcome Tom to the village. One who had been educated in England, explained how honoured Tom's host had felt because Tom had chosen his home. But he was sorry that he had no food in the house. He had killed his pet dog to provide soup for Tom.

To THINK ABOUT

- Think about a time when you felt welcomed into someone's home. What was it that made you feel welcome? What was said? What was done? What the home was like?

- When someone visits you, what do you usually do to make them feel welcome?

WHY THE DIFFERENCE?

Many differences between people groups can be put down to 'culture'. The history of a people makes them think differently and act differently. As you get to know someone of another culture, you will not only find differences in ideas of friendship, but also in how people dress, what they eat and how they treat visitors. There will be different manners, different values and different ideas about how family, community and society should be organised. There will also be different views on how men and women should relate to each other.

Some of these things are historical accidents, but some have to do with religion. In Sikhism, Hinduism and Islam, many aspects of life that Westerners see as personal choice are determined by religion. For example, Westerners see diet as a matter of personal choice. Jesus, we remember, declared all foods 'clean' (Mark 7:19), so that the ethical or religious basis for the choice has to do with general principles like justice, kindness and environmental care. In contrast:

- Islam forbids pork and alcohol, and any product of an animal that has not been killed according to Islamic law.

- Hinduism forbids beef, and many Hindus are strict vegetarians.

- Sikhism forbids alcohol, and many Sikhs are vegetarians.

Friendship, hospitality and family unity may also be important aspects of religion. Muhammad said:

'Gather at your meals, you will be blessed therein.'

And:

'The highest virtue is that a person should be benevolent towards his father's friends and the members of their families.'

Chapter 2

MEETING EACH OTHER

'Ida, I want you to meet Paminder. She is a good cooker.'
   'Cooker? You mean cook! If she's a cooker, we have to put the pans on her to boil!'
   How we laughed!

First meetings can be full of misunderstandings! Not all are as funny as this one. Sometimes, we do not even realise that we have misunderstood each other, with the result that we end up offended or confused. We could try to give a long list of 'do's and don'ts' to help you avoid misunderstandings, but it would not be very helpful. You would not remember them all, and it might make you feel as if every visit to your friend was an exam. It is more helpful simply to remember that there will be differences, and to expect that both you and your friend will have a lot to learn about each other. One thing you will need is a sense of humour – friendships always go quicker if you can laugh together.

EAST MEETS WEST

In the early part of our courtship, Ann's parents invited me for Sunday lunch. The seconds of roast were passed around, and I took only a little as I knew there would be another course. Then I was offered the last piece. 'Go on,' urged Ann's mum. 'I really don't want to save it.' I declined, very politely – or so I thought.

Ann remembers the incident with some dread. It was not that I had taken a second helping. It was not that I hadn't been overawed by meeting her family. It was not even that I had declined that last piece. It was the tone of voice in which I had said, 'No, thank you' that had been the problem.

You see, my grandmother is a typical Indian mother, who enjoys feeding her offspring. She loves cooking for us all. So when I simply say, 'No, thank you', she puts even more on my plate, saying, 'Oh, you can eat it!' It is right in my culture to say, 'No!' and even to take the plate off the table to prevent her from putting more food on it. It was this forceful 'No!' which had come across as rude to Ann's mother and which had embarrassed Ann.'

The challenge for an Easterner entering Western culture is at least as great as that for a Westerner entering Eastern culture. In the above story, it was just that the two cultures have different ways of communicating. For the Indian grandmother, pressing more food on a guest is a way of showing acceptance. 'Don't be shy,' she would say. 'Treat this like your own home.' She would mean, 'Take as much as you want to. And we will make sure that you have everything you need whether you take it or you don't.' It is like a game. The guest will start by taking less that he wants. When seconds are offered he can at first refuse, but will then be able to make his host happy by eating more. When yet more food is offered, he will forcefully insist that he has had enough and that were he to eat more he would burst. Neither Ann nor her mother understood this game; and Ann's fiancé did not realise that there was a different game to be learned.

TO THINK ABOUT
• In your culture, how do you show that you are enjoying a meal? What do you say? What do you do?

- Here are some ways that people of different cultures show appreciation of food. Which ones are offensive in your culture?

  Belching loudly, sweating, eating as much as possible, leaving some of the food uneaten (to announce, 'I'm full up'), asking for the recipe.

Difference goes much deeper than ways of doing things and being polite. When people come from the East to the West, they find not only different customs, but also different ways of thinking. Perhaps the greatest challenge is the little question, 'Why?'

'Why?' is a major source of tension in an Asian family where parents are of one generation and the children of another. The parents' views are formed by the way things were done in their own parents' homes. The children's 'Why?' challenges the authority of the household, not only of the father – the head of the house – but also of the family tradition and the family name. This affects the standing of the family in the community.

The young people are brought up in Western culture, with Western education that teaches them to reason for themselves, so it is not surprising if they want to ask questions at home. Their parents are likely to have been taught to do what they were told. They may have learnt by rote, without understanding, and been taught that teachers are revered gurus who are always right. They simply accepted what the older generation handed on to them.

Family traditions are also handed down: 'This is how it is done.' The question 'Why?' is never asked in important matters. If a rebellious child should ask it, she will be told, 'Just do it.' If your parents wish it, or the teacher or the priest says it, no further questions are needed. Most Asian cultures simply do not have room for the question, 'Why?'

Mr Lal makes light bulbs. He learnt his trade as an apprentice thirty years ago, and still makes the bulbs just as he was taught. Similarly, he was taught his family's religious and cultural rituals by his parents, especially by his mother. His father had married a girl from the same caste, and had inherited some of her family's rituals. He passed the traditions on to his son, Mr Lal, who in turn married a girl from the same caste who brought some of her family rituals with her. Now Mr and Mrs Lal teach their children to continue the traditions passed down from one generation to another.

For example, when Mr Lal's parents were expecting their first child, there was a ritual to ensure the safety of mother and baby. This ritual, slightly updated, was passed on to Mr and Mrs Lal when they were expecting their first baby. When their daughter-in-law was pregnant, the same ritual – again, slightly updated – was passed on to her. Such rituals, customs and values are very important to Asian families.

Sunita, Mr Lal's daughter, recently completed a degree in business and is a sales rep. She has a different outlook on life. She wants reasons for following family customs. Her question, 'Why must it be this way?' causes great tension in the family. Her father cannot answer her because he followed his father's instructions without questioning. He thought that his father knew best, and that he should respect him and learn from him. Living in the UK has helped him to understand Sunita's questions, but he is frustrated that he is not able to answer her. He can only tell her what to do, not why to do it.

Some years ago, a survey was carried out in Bombay. The question went like this: 'The climate in the Northern Hemisphere is generally wet. England is situated in the Northern Hemisphere. London is the capital of England. Generally, what kind of climate would you expect in London?'

The overwhelming reply was 'I don't know. I have never been to London.' People are not brought up to reason, but to accept the word of their elders – their parents, grandparents, teachers, and priests. The young who have gone through the Western education system are a great challenge to their elders, fathers, grandfathers and priests. The elders are facing this challenge in different ways. Some let their children do what they want, some learn to compromise and some fight to keep their ways sacred.

Asians who have been brought up in the West are also facing the challenge in different ways. Some rebel against their family traditions, some reluctantly accept compromise, some reach a balance between Eastern and Western ideas, and some stay within their families, rejecting the West as far as possible.

Asians in Britain have different religions. They come from different ethnic groups and have different languages. They have different levels of education, and come from different social groups. But one of the biggest differences among them is in how they are engaging with the West.

'Do you like curry?' asked Nasma, Amanda's new Indian neighbour. 'Come to my house, any time you like!' Amanda has read about Eastern hospitality, so she chose a meal-time , and went and knocked on the door. Nasma was delighted to see her, and brought her into the sitting room, where the family were eating a curry. The smell was wonderful, and Amanda's mouth was watering. 'Do have some food,' said Nasma. Amanda remembered her manners: 'In an Asian home, it is rude to appear to eager to eat,' her book had said. So she said, 'I'm not really very hungry just at the moment.'
Unfortunately, Nasma had also done her cultural homework. 'These English don't like to be pressed about food,' she knew. 'If they say they don't want any, they mean it.' So she gave Amanda a cup of tea, and Amanda went home two hours later – still hungry.

'What a disappointment!' said Nasma to her husband. 'I thought she liked me enough to want to eat with us!'

To think about
- What mistakes did Amanda and Nasma make?

- What could they have done to clear up their misunderstanding?

WEST MEETS EAST
'How should I approach an Asian?'
   'Hello! How are you?'

As any other relationship, a friendship with an Asian will probably start with a greeting. It might be outside the school gates, in a shop, at the hairdresser, in the street or even at a party. Usually, it will not be a man greeting a woman, or vice versa – in some traditional Asian families, a woman who speaks to a man outside her family is being immodest. If she shakes hands with him, people may be scandalised.

The greeting may be followed by general talk, so that you get to know a little about each other. Exchanging information about families is a good place to start. As you talk, you can find out what you have in common. You can then start to make an effort to meet your friend regularly.

The three stories below tell how some friendships have started. We have chosen them to show how people have had to think about the differences between them. The friends did not start with a lot of knowledge of each other's cultures. They became friends when they tried to understand each other and, maybe more important, when they discovered what they had in common.

A bumpy beginning
Mike had a new neighbour. Looked just like him – right suit, right car, right accent; but he was just a bit

different – he had a brown skin. Mike was a Christian, so he thought he'd make friends with the neighbour, as he would with anyone else. After all, the man might be a Muslim or a Hindu or something, and he'd need to hear the gospel.

'Hello!' he said, as they met outside their front doors one evening. 'I'm Mike, your neighbour. How do you do?' They shook hands, and the neighbour introduced himself. They started chatting – about the weather, the neighbourhood and the latest news.

'What next?' wondered Mike. 'I know – hospitality. I've always heard that these Asians are hospitable.' No sooner thought than done! 'Do come in for a drink, 'he said. 'I usually have a sherry about this time.'

The neighbour looked a little embarrassed. 'No, thank you very much,' he said. 'Please excuse me. I have some work to do.' And he disappeared behind his front door.

To THINK ABOUT

- What did Mike do right?

- What did Mike do wrong?

- What do you think of Mike's attitude to his neighbour?

- How do you think the neighbour might continue the relationship in the future?

Fatima finds a real friend

Fatima is attractive and intelligent, and has plenty of friends at school. She is not very religious, but she does try to keep to her faith. She says her prayers when it is not too inconvenient, she keeps the Ramadan fast every year, and she wouldn't dream of taking pork or alcohol or of having a boy friend.

'My English friends just don't understand,' she says. 'When I tell them I can't come to their parties, they say I'm soft. I should just tell my parents I'm going to the library, they say. The boys are always inviting me out, and are offended when I say no. The worst was during the Gulf War, when everyone was talking about Muslims. "These Muslims are crazy!" they'd say. "They're fanatics. They're always fighting." "Excuse me," I'd say. "I'm a Muslim. Am I always fighting?" I'll never forget Richard's answer. "Oh! I don't think of you as a Muslim. I know you don't come to parties, but otherwise you're just like us.'

'I didn't say anything. I was too angry. I'm not just like them. My home isn't like theirs. They don't know what it's like to have a different language spoken at home, and to eat different food, and to have half your relatives on the other side of the world. They're supposed to be Christians, but most of them don't even believe in God. That makes them different from me for a start!

'The only one who even noticed that I was upset was Judith. She's Afro-Caribbean, and she's a real Christian. She goes to church and she doesn't get drunk or sleep around. "I think I can understand a bit," she said. "I feel bad when they talk about the church. They mock, and they don't know what they're talking about. And Richard is like that about being black too. He just doesn't see that the colour of your skin does make a difference. He doesn't know what it's like when smaller kids call you 'black bastard'. And he's never had the privilege of coming from another culture."

'"Privilege?" I asked. "I suppose it is, isn't it? I know all sorts of things that they don't know. I'd never thought of it that way before."'

That was the start of a beautiful friendship. Judith and Fatima had been part of a group of 'friends'. Now they have started to share what they really feel about life.

TO THINK ABOUT
• Why was Fatima so angry with Richard?

- What difference can a 'real Christian' make in a crowd of friends?

- What sorts of experiences did Judith have to go through so that she could understand Fatima?

- Ask God to lead you into experiences that will give you more in common with your Asian neighbours.

Her daughter goes to the same school

Sharon lives in an inner city area, where people from all sorts of backgrounds live next door to each other. For a long time she felt that she would like to get to know some of the women from other ethnic groups. But most of them couldn't speak English, and she didn't know where to start. So she prayed, and then it happened:

'Mrs Khan organised an Asian week at the school. It was really interesting, and I met Latheefa. One of her daughters was in the same class as my Gemma, so I went to her house. I couldn't talk to her much because her English was not very good – I spent more time with the children – but we became good friends, and I've got to know some other families too. Latheefa never comes to my house, but the children do. They play with my children.

'Some people think the Asians are different, but I've realised that they're just normal human beings. They do some things differently, though. Like, when we have visitors, we stay in the room with them. The Bengalis go in and out and sometimes leave you alone. It was strange when I went to a wedding. The women were huddled in one corner, and the men were in the rest of the room. We were put with the men, and it felt very strange. The bride, who I knew, wasn't even there – she was at home.

'One of my children really likes Latheefa's lentil curry. I've often eaten there. They used to bring me a knife and fork, but then I saw that they all ate with their fingers. You never think of that – you just assume everyone uses a knife and fork – well, you know the Chinese use chopsticks. But it's really quite hygienic when you wash your hands first, and it makes it much easier to eat fish and things like that – you can feel the bones! I made a terrible mess when I first tried, and we had a good laugh, but I'm quite good at it now. I've learnt to eat with the right hand – it's rude to use the left one, isn't it?

'I did stop visiting for a while. The teenage daughter was in a bad mood, and she was very rude to me and told me to stop coming. I told her that it wouldn't make any difference to my friendship with her mother, but I didn't go back for a while. When I did, it was OK again, and the daughter apologised. I told her I'd forgiven her and to forget it. It's been fine since then.'

TO THINK ABOUT

- What things made it difficult for Sharon to make friends with Latheefa?

- What attitudes in Sharon made the friendship possible?

- What have Sharon and her family gained through knowing Latheefa?

- How do you think Latheefa might describe the friendship?

These three stories are about different people in different situations. The Christians described are different: male and female, black and white, younger and older, more educated and less educated. The Asians described are also different.

Friends may have more in common with each other than with other Asians or even other Christians. God made us different – he likes us that way.

If you have not yet found a friend, you can always ask God to lead you to someone of his choice.

Back in 1996, someone in our men's group had a mental picture of 'a man of peace' on a certain road near a supermarket. ('A man of peace' is a reference to Jesus' words in Matthew 10:11–13, someone in whom God is at work, who will respond warmly to Christians.)

I spent some time walking up and down the road, asking the Lord who this person was, and the group kept on praying for him. About nine months later, I had a sense that it was a Hindu man who owned a launderette. We prayed for him, and I discovered that a couple from the church also knew him. I have started going to this launderette to do my washing, and am slowly getting to know this man. We often talk about God.

God leads different people in different ways. There are people living near you in whom God is working already. He wants them to have Christian friends.

THINKING ABOUT THIS SECTION

- Look back over the stories of Mike, Fatima, Sharon and 'the man of peace'. Which of the people in the stories are like you? Which are like people you know?

- What have you found in these stories to encourage you in your friendships with people of other faiths?

- Your church secretary says, 'I think we should have some outreach to the Asian people in our area.' Make a list of ideas you could give him/her, to get the church started. Here are two to get *you* started:

    Find out who has Asian friends already, and pray for them.

    Invite an Asian friend to a home group, to tell them what it feels like to be Asian and living in your area.

Chapter 3

WHAT THE BIBLE SAYS

RUTH: CROSS-CULTURAL FRIENDSHIPS

The Book of Ruth tells the wonderful story of how a foreign woman, with a different religion, trusted the God of Israel, became part of the people of Israel and took a key role in the history of Israel.

Jewish people read Ruth's story every year at the time of Rejoicing over Torah, which comes after the feast of Shavuot (Pentecost). They remember how this Gentile woman came to love the Torah, the law God had given to Israel. As far as we know, Ruth never attended an evangelistic meeting or received a tract. It all happened through ordinary human relationships, including a tragic loss, a faithful friendship and a romantic marriage. (We suggest you read the Bible story before continuing with the rest of this chapter. It's in the Old Testament; using the Contents list in your Bible will help you find it quickly.)

TO THINK ABOUT AS YOU READ THE STORY

- Ruth is a bit like some of the Asian women in Britain. How does her story help us to understand them?

- Naomi is the believer, from the people of God. Ruth is from another faith and culture. How does their relationship grow?

- Sometimes people see more of God in what we do than in what we say. In what ways does Boaz act like Jesus?

The story

To begin with, it was not Ruth who was foreign, but rather the Jewish family who came as refugees to her country, Moab. Ruth was married to one of their sons. In that culture, as in many Asian cultures today, this meant that she became part of his family and lived with him in his parents' home.

What did she think of her husband and her new family? We are not told. Some Asian women in Britain arrive here after being married to strangers who came from overseas with their families. These families, settled in Britain, take their sons back to their villages in India, Bangladesh or Pakistan to find brides. The new wife may then return to Britain with them, separated from her own parents, her brothers and sisters, and her friends. More likely, the groom and his family will return to Britain without her, and there will be a long wait – perhaps several years – until she gets permission from the Home Office to join him.

In some ways, life was easier for Ruth. She expected to stay in her own country, near to her own family. Israel was not so far from Moab as Britain is from Pakistan. Moabite as well as Israelite life depended on agriculture.

In other ways, life must have been more difficult for her. A man brought up in Britain will have picked up many Western ways of thinking, but at least he will be from the same ethnic group. He will also have the same religion as his bride. For Ruth, marriage meant going into a home with a different culture and a different god. She must have found all the laws about what to eat, how to be clean and when to worship strange and confusing.

Asian women brought to Britain from their own countries react to their marriages in different ways. Some are happy, some are sad, and some are simply confused. Few have much time to think about it – although some are engaged months before marriage, the time from first contact to the wedding may be as short as two weeks – and the girl may have little choice but to accept her parents' decision.

So, we don't know how the marriage happened, whether Ruth had any say in it, or how she felt about it. But we do know that she was spared the prospect of leaving her country and living far from her family. But things did not turn out as she expected.

A tragic loss

Women need men. In Moab and Israel, as well as in most Asian cultures, a woman on her own is very vulnerable. She has no protector: no one to give her a home, no one to provide for her, no one to speak for her.

Naomi had lost her husband, but at least she had her sons left. They married, and she expected soon to have grandsons, who would guarantee peace in her old age. Then tragedy struck. Both sons died before grandsons could be born. Now she had no male protector, and she had responsibility for two young women – her sons' wives.

What was Naomi to do? She had no relatives in Moab – her family were in Israel. She had been away for ten years, and there was no email or even Royal Mail in those days. Yet perhaps they would remember her and welcome her back. There were, she remembered, laws about looking after the poor and the widows in Israel. So she decided to go back.

But what about her daughters-in-law? As long as they stayed with her, she was responsible for them. She was not even sure that she would be able to provide for herself in Israel, so she decided to send them back to their own families. One agreed. The other, Ruth, refused because of her devotion to Naomi.

To think about

- Make a list of things in South Asian culture that are like Old Testament culture.

- The death of a husband or wife is said to be one of the most difficult bereavements. What things in Naomi's circumstances made the loss of her husband especially difficult?

- Imagine that you are Naomi, deciding whether to take your daughters-in-law back to Israel. What makes you want to take them? What makes you want to leave them behind? What would be best for them?

An extraordinary friendship

Naomi thought she was being a friend to Ruth by sending her back to her parents. That was ordinary friendship: she wanted Ruth to be safe in a familiar place, while she herself went into the unknown.

The extraordinary friendship was not shown by Naomi, the Jewish believer, but by Ruth, the Gentile. Ruth loved her mother-in-law, and insisted on going with her. She didn't know what might happen to her. She had never been to Israel, and had never seen whether the social security system there worked. Yet she would not leave this sad, vulnerable woman alone. Here is what she said:

> 'Don't urge me to leave you or to turn back from you. Where you go I will go, and where you stay I will stay. Your people will be my people and your God my God. Where you die I will die, and there I will be buried. May the Lord deal with me, be it ever so severely, if anything but death separates you and me.' *(Ruth 1:16–18)*

What a statement of friendship!

Ruth will stay with Naomi. She will always be there for her.

Ruth will become part of Naomi's people. She will take on a different culture for Naomi's sake.

Ruth commits herself to Naomi. A friend, she believes, is for life.

Ruth even commits herself to Naomi's religion.

Was she already a believer? We do not know. We know that she must have conformed to her new family's way of life, but we do not know what she herself believed. Most people at the time thought that each god had power in a particular place, so by leaving Moab Ruth was also leaving the Moabite gods. However she understood it, she decided to join Naomi's people, and this would mean accepting Naomi's God.

TO THINK ABOUT

- From what you know of your Asian friend's culture, how much of it can you share without being disloyal to Christ?

- Imagine you are Naomi again, and you have told Ruth and Orpah your decision to go away. Listen to their responses to your suggestion that they go home. How do they make you feel?

- A friend from another culture can be a wonderful gift from God.

A romantic marriage

The two women arrive in Israel and go to Bethlehem, Naomi's home village. We are not told how they find shelter, but we are told how they find food. They use the law that provides for poor people to pick up whatever is left in the fields after the harvest.

Ruth happens to choose a field that belongs to Boaz, one of her husband's relatives. Again, we are not told how this happens. It seems to be mere chance, but we wonder whether God is leading her.

Now, we see Boaz offering friendship to the foreign woman (Ruth 2). He does not acknowledge his relationship to her. He is a rich man, and perhaps he does not want to take responsibility for two destitute women. But he does notice her and treat her well:

> He welcomes her. He invites her to stay in his field and not go elsewhere (v 8).

> He knows she has no male protector, so he protects her. He tells his workmen not to harass her (v 9).

> He respects her. He speaks to her not as a foreigner, but as 'My daughter' (v 8).

> He offers hospitality. She can have a drink of water whenever she likes (v 9), and she is even invited to stay for lunch (vs 14–15).

> He provides for her. He tells the harvesters to make sure they leave grain for her to pick up (vs 15–16).

Ruth is surprised! 'Why have I found such favour in your eyes?' she asks. 'You notice me – a foreigner.' Was Boaz already attracted to her, we wonder? Or was he easing his conscience, thinking that perhaps he should offer her and Naomi a home? Perhaps there was a bit of both. We only know his reply:

> 'I've been told all about what you have done for your mother-in-law since the death of your husband – how you left your father and mother and your homeland and came to live with a people you did not know before.' *(v 11)*

Whatever his inner thoughts, Boaz had heard about Ruth.

He knew about her extraordinary friendship, about her difficulties and about the sacrifices she had made. So he goes on:

> 'May the Lord repay you for what you have done. May you be richly rewarded by the Lord, the God of Israel, under whose wings you have come to take refuge.' *(v 12)*

This, it seems, is Boaz's answer to Ruth's question. He is a believer in the living God. He knows that God has seen Ruth. He knows that God understands all her difficulties. He prays that God will bless her. Boaz, as God's man, is working with God. There was no point in his praying for God to bless Ruth if he wasn't going to bring her blessing himself.

In the end, Boaz gets his reward too – Ruth is so obedient to Naomi that she is willing to marry him. Boaz gets a good wife, and he takes up his responsibility towards his relatives.

Again, we do not know how the various parties felt. We do know that Ruth and Naomi were given security and that the family received the blessing of a child. Now Naomi had her grandson, Obed. God replaced all that they had lost.

Ruth's friendship with Naomi brought blessings to all, and this poor foreigner became a key figure in God's plan for his people and his world. Her son, Obed, would be the grandfather of the great King David, from whose lineage would come the Messiah.

TO THINK ABOUT

- Why was Ruth surprised when Boaz showed friendship towards her?

- Are things very different for people from ethnic minorities in your town today?

- List the ways in which Boaz showed friendship towards Ruth. Can any of them be applied to your friendships with Hindus, Muslims or Sikhs?

A challenge for our churches

Ruth had already come to join the people of God when Boaz met her, and she had left her family to do it. People from Hindu, Sikh and Muslim families sometimes lose their homes when they come to Christ. They need new families and they need marriage partners. What kind of friendship do we offer them?

IDEA

Read the story of Ruth (or watch the *Testament* video)* with an Asian friend. He or she may like to tell you where there are similarities between Ruth's culture and his or her own. You could also discuss how welcome Asians feel in Britain.

EATING TOGETHER: A BIBLE THEME

Sharing meals is a mark of friendship in Asian cultures, and was a mark of friendship in Bible times too. It is even a mark of our friendship with God. If we 'share salt' with people, we are treating them as God treats us. This study looks at some of the important meals in the Bible. (It would be helpful to read the Bible passage first, then to go through the comments in this book and, finally, to re-read the passage.)

Abraham shared salt with angels (Genesis 18:1–8)

The letter to the Hebrews tells us: 'Do not forget to entertain strangers, for by doing so some people have entertained angels without knowing it' (13:2). The writer must have been thinking of Abraham's experience here in Genesis.

Abraham was sitting in front of his tent when he saw three men approaching. He welcomed them according to the customs of his people:

He went out to them and bowed to them.

He invited them in.

He told them that they would be doing him a favour by eating with him.

He spoke of himself as their 'servant'.

He brought them water, so that they could wash and have a drink. It was the middle of the day, so they must have been thirsty and dusty.

He roused his household, and got together the best meal possible.

He stood over them while they ate.

All this is very like Asian hospitality. The guest is honouring the host, and the host has responsibilities to the guest. Like an Indian grandmother, Abraham watches over their every need and urges them to eat more until there is nothing left. The rest of the chapter tells us that Abraham was indeed honoured by his visitors. They were angels, and one is even called 'the Lord' (v10).

TO THINK ABOUT

- How does Abraham's hospitality compare with the way you usually treat guests? What things in your culture make you act differently?

- How does this story help you to understand what might be going on when you visit Asian friends?

- Discuss with an Asian friend whether or not it would be helpful to alter your customs to meet their needs when they come to you, and vice versa.

Gideon shared salt with the Lord (Judges 6:17–24)

The angel of the Lord appeared to Gideon and told him to lead a battle to free the Israelites from the Midianites.

Gideon was not sure about this. He wanted to be certain that the command was from God. So he asked the angel to wait while he prepared a meal. Then he brought bread and meat and laid them out for his visitor.

The angel accepted Gideon's invitation. He told Gideon to put the meal on a rock and to pour out the gravy. Then he touched the food with his stick, and it was consumed by fire. The angel disappeared, but Gideon was sure that he had met with God himself. He built an altar called 'The Lord is Peace'. God had accepted his offering of food, so Gideon knew that he had 'found favour' with him (v 17). Frightened, ordinary Gideon would have the Lord as his friend.

To think about

- What do you think was in Gideon's mind when he prepared the food for the angel?

- The Lord accepted Gideon's hospitality. How did this help Gideon:

  – in his attitude to himself?

  – in his understanding of God?

  – in his response to God's call?

Jesus shared salt with sinners

Jesus started his public ministry by going to a meal (John 2:1–11). He sealed his relationship with his first disciples by going to eat in their home (Mark 1:29–31). He spent his last night with his disciples sharing a meal and, at that final gathering, he assured them that they were his friends (John 15:13–17). After his resurrection, he ate with them (Luke 24:30, 41–43; John 21:9–13). Again and again, Jesus showed his love for people by sharing salt with them. He was their friend.

Sometimes he was criticised for his friendships. The religious leaders accused him of dining with the wrong people. They complained, 'Here is a drunkard and a glutton, a friend of tax collectors and sinners' (Luke 7:34).

Jews at the time of Jesus divided the world into two groups: themselves and the rest. The Jews were made distinct from the rest by the laws given to them through Abraham and Moses. They were circumcised, they kept the Sabbath and they ate nothing 'unclean'. They had been chosen by God to be his special people.

There were, of course, some Jews who did not keep the laws. Worse still, there were some who were friends with the Roman occupiers. Pious Jews thought that these people were betraying Israel. They were disqualifying themselves from being part of the true people of God. They were known as 'sinners'.

There was, of course, truth in this. The Old Testament teaches that the blessings of the covenant are for those who keep the law; those who break it are under a curse (see Deuteronomy 27–30). That the land of Israel was being ruled by the Romans was evidence that the Jews had been unfaithful to God, so pious Jews were eager to reverse this situation (eg Daniel 9:7). They tried hard to keep the law themselves and shunned those who did not.

Jesus flouted their rules: he let a sinful woman touch him (Luke 7:39); he even went to the home of a notorious sinner and ate with him (Luke 5:29). It is not surprising that the religious leaders were angry. Levi was a traitor to Israel because he collected taxes for the Romans: by sharing a meal with him, Jesus was honouring him.

Levi was not the only 'sinner' whom Jesus honoured. He went to eat with Zacchaeus (Luke 19:1–10). This time he took the initiative and invited himself. Zacchaeus would never have had the courage to ask such a holy person to his house: he would have feared rejection.

Why did Jesus eat with these people? He explained:

'It is not the healthy who need a doctor, but the sick. I have not come to call the righteous, but sinners to repentance.' *(Luke 5:31–32)*

'The Son of Man came to seek and to save what
was lost.' *(Luke 19:10)*

By accepting their hospitality, Jesus was publicly declaring
that these outcasts were his friends.

TO THINK ABOUT

- Look up the word 'eat' in a concordance and find the
  references in the gospels. Why do you think there is so
  much about eating?

- Read Luke 19:1–10 again. Close your eyes and imagine
  what it might be like to be Zacchaeus … Usually no one
  wants to visit your home … You really want to see Jesus,
  but dare not invite him … Jesus tells you he is coming to
  visit you … Now he is coming into your home … What do
  you feel? What will you do?

Peter didn't want to share salt with a foreigner (Acts 10)

Peter had spent three years with Jesus. He had seen him eating with 'sinners' and had probably eaten with them himself. But he didn't realise that he should also eat with
Gentiles. The Jews, he thought, should keep themselves
clean, and Gentiles ate unclean food.

God thought differently. He always intended to have one
human family belonging to himself. This family would
include Gentiles as well as Jews. Heaven is described as a
wedding feast, where we will all eat together and no one will
be 'unclean' (Revelation 19:9; Matthew 22:1–14). Peter
needed a direct lesson from God before he understood this.

By the end of Acts 10, Peter's attitude is very different
from what it was at the beginning. The change was so
important that the story is recounted again in the very next
chapter.

To THINK ABOUT
- What did Peter learn? List the various stages in Peter's learning experience. For each stage:

  What did God do?

  What did Peter do?

  What did Peter learn?

- Peter thought that Cornelius was 'unclean'. What did God think of Cornelius?

- The problem in bringing Cornelius to Christ was not in Cornelius but in Peter. What things in ourselves and in our churches prevent Asians from hearing the gospel?

Jesus offers to share salt with us

One of the best known verses in the Bible is Revelation 3:20: 'Here I am! I stand at the door and knock. If anyone hears my voice and opens the door…' We often hear this as a call to open our lives to Jesus and a promise that he will come in. In the West, we seldom notice what it is that he plans to do when he enters: 'I will come in and eat with him, and he with me'.

To THINK ABOUT
- How does this study on eating help you understand Revelation 3:20?

- Think about the Asian ideas of sharing salt, outlined in chapter 2. What might Jesus' offer of friendship mean to your Asian friend?

Jesus wants to be the guest, to bring honour and be loyal to your Asian friend. He also wants to be the host, to give honour and loyalty to your friend. Once this favour is accepted, brotherhood with Jesus is sealed. All the hosts of heaven will see that your friend is part of Jesus' family. He will never let your friend down.

Jesus died and rose again so that he can eat with your friend and your friend can eat with him.

IDEAS

• Use these studies in your home group.

• Invite some Hindu, Muslim or Sikh friends to study some of these passages with you and some Christian friends. Ask them to share what 'eating together' means in their faiths.

Note

* The story of Ruth is beautifully retold on video, *Testament*: see 'Further Resources'.

Chapter 4

TAKING IT DEEPER

Friendships deepen as we spend time together. With Asians, this is likely to mean spending time in peoples' homes and getting to know their families. In general, people will be happier if you visit their home than if you invite them to yours. (Although some families have adjusted to Western patterns of hospitality, many will expect you to 'drop in' withouth an invitation.) In the West, you honour people by inviting them to a meal. In the East, you honour people by visiting their home and accepting food from them.

You may also find that your friend gives you gifts. In some Asian cultures, relationships are sealed by gifts. If you want to continue a relationship, you give something. The friend then gives you something of a slightly higher value. Next time, you give something worth a little more again. That is why you may see someone writing down how much is given by the different guests at weddings. The families want to give the right amount at the next occasion.

As gifts and hospitality are given and received, the friends get to know each other. They learn about each other's faiths, families and cultures. They find out more about how they are different, but share more of what they have in common. Whatever their differences, the friends are human. They start to share feelings, are able to disagree with each other, and get involved in each other's concerns. It is at this stage that they may begin to feel part of each other's families.

Many friendships start with great excitement:

'They are so hospitable.'

'I love the food.'

'I was so touched when she sent me a card for our festival.'

'The wedding was so interesting – the customs are so different from ours.'

But most friendships also go through patches where we wonder whether it is all worthwhile. Does the other person really want to be friends at all? We have chosen the stories in this chapter to encourage you to keep on loving your friend, whatever happens. It is our experience that as we pray and persevere, we come through such patches bound together in stronger and richer relationships.

JOHN: DEVELOPING TRUST

'Let's call him Mushtaq, but then let's also call him Mush because I know him by his short name. He's in his late teens, and is a Mirpuri in a city where the Mirpuris are scattered rather than living in a close community. He would describe his language as Urdu, but his spoken version seems to have little in common with the written language.

'I know Mush through being a neighbour and "roping him in" for the occasional cricket match. Cricket is his sport, and when we get together – which is not often, owing to the pressures of life – cricket is the topic of conversation. I wouldn't push the gospel at him any more than I would with my other male friends who are ethnically English.

'I feel for Mush in that he seems to have the same self-contained, wary attitudes that I had as a teenager. I think being brought up as a Muslim must be quite similar to being brought up as a teetotal, television-free, non-swearing, Sabbath-observing Methodist – as I was. I have known him turn down an entire cricket tea because it was obvious that there was ham on the plate for one course. I tried to get an alternative for him, but they just weren't prepared for a Muslim. Turning down a cricket tea must spoil your entire outing. How restricted and isolated he must feel at times! With such a background, one needs a safe topic of conversation like cricket before one can open up.

'So that's where Mush and me are – we meet occasionally, have a friendly chat, and we care about each other.'

TO THINK ABOUT

• What sorts of things have helped Mush and John to trust each other?

• Why might cricket be more appealing to Mush than football? (Think who has done well in cricket in the past few years!)

> **Jesus helps people to trust him**
> *Matthew 14:22–33;*
> *Mark 8:22–26;*
> *John 14:1*
> What makes it difficult to trust? How does Jesus help us to trust?

• Where have Mush and John had to persevere with each other?

CLAIRE: VISITING

'I feel so encouraged by their hospitality. They really take trouble. Naseem even sends one of the children round to the baker's if she has nothing nice to give me when I drop in. I wouldn't do that – I'd just give her what I happened to have in the house!

'I'm the sort of person who feels apprehensive when I visit people – I'm not sure they really want me. But my Asian friends welcome me, even though I'm from a different culture. They seem to accept me, and even to need me. I'm not particularly brilliant at English, but Naseem says I've helped her. It's nice to feel that I have something to offer.

'Of course, there are some things that make me feel awkward. For example, I feel easier if I'm wearing trousers in their homes. I usually wear skirts, but I sometimes feel as if they are looking down on me if I dress normally. Then there's the language barrier. I can communicate quite well with Naseem, but her friend Farzana doesn't know much English, so sometimes I just sit in Farzana's house and drink tea and we don't talk much. Sometimes, she will leave me alone while she gets on with the housework and the children will run around or watch the television – they act almost as if I'm not there at all! In a way, that's nice – it means she doesn't feel she has to stand on ceremony with me. But it's so different from the way we do things at home.

'The women don't often come to visit me – they don't seem to feel at ease in my house. Some won't eat anything except fruit. They think my food might be "unclean".

'The children come though, and sometimes the teenage girls. They can tell me about things they don't want to share with their parents. Shabana comes to play with my Tracey, and I want to encourage that. But sometimes it's disruptive. The other day, she came just as I was about to give Tracey her bath and put her to bed. Shabana doesn't seem to have a bed time!

'I have to admit that I was quite annoyed. My life tends to be very organised – I have a timetable for every day. God helped me to put it aside, and to think, "It doesn't matter if Tracey doesn't have her bath until tomorrow. It doesn't matter if she goes to bed a little bit late tonight."

'Now, even if Shabana arrives as we are sitting down for a meal, I just welcome her in and let her play while we eat. I'm learning to set aside whatever I'm doing when her mum knocks on the door too. Welcoming a person into my home really is more important than getting my jobs done, isn't it?'

TO THINK ABOUT

- What have Claire, Naseem and Farzana gained from their friendship?

- What are the cultural barriers that Claire has had to cross in order to be friends with Naseem and Farzana?

- Why might a Muslim, a Hindu or a Sikh feel uncomfortable in a Christian home?

> **Jesus makes himself at home with different people**
> *Luke 5:27–32; 7:36–50; 10:38–42; 19:1–9; John 4:1–26*
> What were the social and cultural barriers between Jesus and these people? How did he deal with them?

- What do you think of the way that Claire has adapted to Asian ideas about time? Are there other ways of dealing with this cultural difference?

SARAH: THE DEMANDS OF FRIENDSHIP

'Hafeeza's husband makes life difficult for her. He usually looks after the family finances, but sometimes he goes to Bangladesh for months and leaves his wife and children to cope. He never helps with housework, even though he is unemployed and his wife is often ill. The oldest girl is only thirteen, and her older brother is as unhelpful as his father.

'So Hafeeza needs help. And she is not shy to ask for it. "Can you find someone to help my children with their reading? Please help me – I haven't enough money to pay my phone bill! My new vacuum cleaner is broken, and I daren't tell my husband or he'll be angry. My cat is pregnant: what shall I do with the kittens?"

'One day, when she really was too ill to do any housework, she rang me up. "Come and iron a shirt for my husband," she pleaded. "My daughter can't do it well enough to please him, and I'm in too much pain to do it myself. He'll be so angry if there's nothing for him to wear. He's going to meet some important friends."

'"What shall I say?" the thoughts flashed through my mind. "What's going on? Is she treating me as a sister or as a slave? Have I been wrong all along, trying to help Hafeeza every time she's asked me? Have I just been giving her husband an extra woman to do what he wants? I just don't understand. Help me, Lord!"'

To THINK ABOUT

- How would you feel in Sarah's place? Do you think she has been 'wrong all along'? How could she have acted differently?

> **Jesus copes with people's demands**
> *Mark 1:35–45; 3:7–19,31–35; 5:24–34; 6:45–46*
> What sorts of pressure is Jesus under? What different things help him to cope? Why does he react in different ways to different situations?

- List the different ways in which Sarah could answer Hafeeza. For each way, think:

How would this help Hafeeza?

What effect might it have on the rest of her family?

What effect might it have on Sarah?

What might it do to the friendship?

Could it bring honour to Jesus?

STEVE: DISCOVERING HIS FRIEND'S DEEP NEEDS

'I first met Tony three years ago, when he brought his daughter to the church play-group. After a brief introduction, he was willing for me to visit him at home: his wife worked, and he looked after his child. This is not an arrangement favoured by most middle-aged Asian men!

'Tony had lost his first wife to cancer and, in her memory, had built a small school for poor children in India. He was a man of principle and had a "heart for the poor". At first, he was very willing to talk about religion, especially his distrust and dislike of Muslims. As a Rajput Gujurati Hindu, he supported the nationalist movement in India and warned me that the Muslims would soon take over the UK and turn it into an Islamic state. It was real "rivers of blood" stuff! I found this frustrating, as we spent little time talking about spiritual issues. I had to pray hard, too, so that I would not join his criticism of Muslims but speak consistently of God's love for them. For over two years, my occasional visits ended up discussing the same old chestnuts.

'Yet slowly our relationship changed. Tony would often ring me up if I didn't visit and he even came to visit me. Little by little, he admitted his real concerns and emotions. His anger was not so much against the Muslims as against God: he couldn't believe in a loving God because his wife had suffered so much with cancer.

'Two events stand out during this time – the first when I helped him fit a boiler one afternoon. This provoked a real sense of gratitude and trust – Tony confided that most of the Asians he worked for "ripped him off", but the Christians were prompt payers and even tipped him! The second was nine months ago, when he discovered he had Parkinson's disease. Now he has become so desperate for a cure that he invited my pastor and me to visit, pray for healing and anoint him with oil.

'These days our conversation is heart-to-heart and without pretence. We talk about life after death and what will happen to his six-year old daughter when he dies. I pray when he does it will be as a Christian, and that God's healing will extend his life to allow this to happen.

'These three years have sometimes seemed such a long time, especially during the periods of sterile political debate. But I see that those years are nothing compared to eternity, which is perilously close for Tony, whose life seems like a fleeting moment.'

> **Jesus responds to 'sterile debate'**
> *John 4:9–26; 9:1–7;*
> *Luke 9:46–50;*
> *18:18–25; 24:13–35;*
> *Matthew 12:1–45;*
> *15:1–20*
> Look for the standard 'debate' questions in these passages. How does Jesus go behind the questions to what really matters? Notice how he determines whether or not the questioner is genuine.

TO THINK ABOUT

• Why do you think Steve found the political discussions so difficult? How do you think Tony felt about them?

• What kept the friendship going?

• Thinking about the friendships that mean most to you: what has kept them going through the difficult times? Have the difficulties deepened the friendships, or spoilt them?

IDEA

• Read this chapter with someone else who has a friend from another faith.

- Share your experiences of eating in your friends' homes, and of giving or being given gifts.

  What have your friends in common with Mush, Hafeeza, Naseem, Farzana, Shabana and Tony?

  What has been difficult?

  What has been joyful?

Chapter 5

SHARING THE GOSPEL

Hindus, Sikhs and Muslims may find Christianity very strange. The gospel is good news for them, but it may not make sense to begin with. That is because they already have ideas about God and what he expects from them. They also already have ideas about Jesus, and may know quite a lot about him from their own point of view.

- Muslims know about Jesus as a *prophet*. They believe that he is one of many prophets who came to different people at different times in history, bringing the same basic message – the message of Islam. They learn that he was born of a virgin, that he did miracles, that God took him up to heaven and that he will come back again before the end of the world. They also learn that he is not God's Son and that he did not die on the cross.

- Hindus may think of Jesus as an *avatar:* that is, he is a manifestation of God, just like Krishna and the other deities. They may like his teaching – the Sermon on the Mount was made famous by Gandhi. They often criticise Christians for not following what Jesus taught.

- Sikhs think of Jesus as a *guru*. They believe that he was an enlightened religious teacher, just like their ten gurus. They are happy to encourage Christians to follow him, and many like to hear stories about him. They have a tradition of martyrdom and can appreciate Jesus as a leader who died for his people. But they find the idea that he is the one way to God offensive.

Gandhi was once asked by a missionary, 'How can we make Christianity naturalised in India, not a foreign thing, identified with a foreign government and foreign people?'

Gandhi replied, 'First, I would suggest that all of you Christians, missionaries and all, must begin to live more like Jesus Christ. Second, practise your religion without adulterating it or toning it down. Third, emphasise love and make it your working force, for love is central to Christianity. Fourth, study the non-Christian religions more sympathetically to find the good that is within them, in order to have a more sympathetic approach to the people' (from *Gandhi – Portrayal of a friend*, by E Stanley Jones).

As your Asian friend gets to know you, he or she will slowly begin to understand how you think. As you become less of a stranger, your faith will seem less strange. Little by little, you will be able to talk quite naturally about what God is doing for you day by day. You will also be able to discuss each other's beliefs, and be challenged to learn how your friend thinks. You may even find that she wants to convert you! At first, you will probably find her faith just as strange as she finds yours.

You may feel that all the religious rituals are simply wrong. It may help to see some similar ideas in the Bible. This will not only help you see in what ways your friend's beliefs are pointing towards the truth: it will also make you ask which of the things you do are really Christian and which are just part of your culture.

The Book of Leviticus is not popular reading amongst

Christians, but it contains many things of interest to people of other faiths. It describes how God's people are to live in the promised land. They will be known as the Lord's special people, and he wants to make sure that they live up to this. They are to show all the nations what God is like and be a credit to him. Like children, they need to be taught social graces, manners and rules to live by, both in relation to each other and to God, so Moses is given instructions on how they are to conduct their lives:

• Religious and social life is to be organised around festivals, such as Passover which reminds them of their history, Pentecost which reminds them of God's provision, the Jubilee which ensures social justice, and the Sabbath which brings worship into the centre of their lives (ch 23–27).

• There are detailed instructions about worship, offerings and sacrifices, and about the priests who carry out the rituals (ch 1–7).

• There is much about purity – the purity and holiness required of the priests (ch 9–10, 21), clean and unclean foods (ch 11), purification after childbirth (ch 12), rules about diseases (ch 13–14), bodily cleanness (ch 15) and cleansing people to appear before God on the day of Atonement (ch 16).

• There are sexual taboos and various moral laws (ch 18–20).

The laws deal with hygiene, diet, sickness, social order, birth, marriage, death, crime and punishment and economic and social justice, as well as what we might call 'religion'.

Christians tend not to follow these laws: all the details have, we believe, been fulfilled in Jesus. We need to observe the principles behind the laws, but we no longer have to follow the detailed rules. Some of us go so far as to think that such things as diet and hygiene have nothing to do with our faith. However, Leviticus reminds us that God is concerned about the whole of our lives.

Muslims, Hindus and Sikhs also see faith as concerning the whole of life. They have many rules about worship, festivals, home, hygiene, food and social organisation, and what is 'clean' and what is 'unclean'. Life in a traditional Jewish home and life in a traditional Hindu home can be remarkably similar.

The Goldsmiths were giving a party. They decided to hire caterers, but had first to give strict instructions. Neither they nor their guests would be able to eat if everything was not Kosher. And they would have to buy a whole new set of saucepans if the wrong ones were used. The caterers had to be told how, where and when to wash utensils used for foods containing milk products and how, where and when to wash utensils used for meat dishes. And, of course, they had to use the right kinds of food (this comes from Deuteronomy 14:21b). 'Would the young caterer be able to cope?' worried the Goldsmiths.

'No problem,' he said. 'My mother organises her home a bit like that.' His family was from the Vaishnavaa strand of Hinduism, which has strict ceremonial rules. They had a room in their house specially set apart as a shrine to Krishna. It was a holy place, which only believers could enter. Before entering, they would bathe and put on clean clothes. On entering, they would wake the gods, put clothes on them, play with them, sing to them, talk to them, pray to them, wash and do all the chores, as they would for their family. This included cooking for them, using special, set-apart utensils. He could certainly understand the concept of separating things and following religious codes.

Muslims and Hindus (and some Sikhs) follow cleanliness rituals after childbirth, menstruation and sexual activity. Both religions perform ablutions before worship. Both have annual festivals that have particular rituals associated with them. For both, births, marriages and deaths are surrounded by religious traditions.

Hindus also understand the idea of being 'set apart', separate, and ceremonially clean for important religious rituals. They have ceremonies to appease the gods, which have some things in common with the sacrifices described in Leviticus. And they hold to the idea of a priestly caste of families with the specific duty of carrying out religious rituals.

All these are part of life in an Asian home. They are not just meaningless rituals, but ways in which people are seriously trying to relate to God as they understand him. Leviticus can help us to understand this and to invite our friends to go further.

The Lord gave his all to bring his people from slavery in Egypt to freedom in Christ. We can regard the laws of Leviticus as pointing to a way of restoring and maintaining the relationship between the people, or the individual, and God. This restoration took many years, even generations, before Christ the Saviour came. As we seek to lead our Asian friends into full knowledge and restoration with God in Christ, we will have to work just as hard as God did with his people Israel. We can find pointers to Christ in their beliefs and rituals; little by little, we will be able to help them see their need for the Saviour, and introduce them to him.

- As we share our lives, and the stories of Jesus, we will be able to help our friends to see what true, inner cleanness is about. The Holy Spirit will show them how impossible it is to make themselves truly clean.

- As they see what our Lord has done for us, we will help them to hope that they, too, can know Jesus in a new way.

They will understand that he wants to be their friend. Then the cross and the resurrection will really be good news to them.

To think about
Think back over what you have read in this book, then consider your friendships with people of different faiths:

- What has challenged your own faith?

- Where have you seen truth and goodness in people of other faiths?

- What difference does Jesus make to you? What aspects of your faith do you want to thank God for?

- Why do you want to share the gospel with your friends?

SPEAKING ABOUT THE GOSPEL

Listening is an important part of any relationship. As we listen to each other, we find out what really matters to our friends and share with them what really matters to us. Some of us will find this easier than others!

For Bruce, sharing the gospel came quite naturally. He writes:

'Chan was born in Uganda, and his family were Hindu. Having spent most of his life in this country however, he was secular in outlook and agnostic in religious belief. We both started new jobs at about the same time. He was my line manager. For some reason, we seemed to hit it off very quickly.

'Once a week we would take lunch together at a local pub and chat about work, football, but more often than not, social issues. Chan was a committed Socialist, and although my Christian faith meant that we came at issues from different starting points, we shared a common passion for justice. As a result, Christ very naturally came into our discussions. That the Bible had something relevant to say about some of the issues we were discussing seemed to surprise and intrigue him. Maybe it was this that caused him, as our relationship developed, to begin asking me more direct questions about my Christian faith.

'After three years working together, he moved on to a better job elsewhere. However, we kept in touch, and from time to time we would meet up with him and his wife. Very recently, he asked me if I could recommend a book which introduced the Christian faith.

'As I look back over our relationship, it is clear that God has been using the natural setting of our relationship, and the common ground we have within it, to encourage Chan to look more closely at the person of Christ.'

For Claire, things were different:

'When I first started visiting my Muslim neighbours, I felt I had to "witness" every time, so I kept looking for opportunities and saying things even when there wasn't really an opening. I don't do that any more. I don't worry if we only talk about the children. And it's funny, but I seem to have more opportunities now. The women are always asking me about my lifestyle – my prayers, whether I drink alcohol, how I teach my daughter. They're really interested.

They don't often ask about Jesus, though. The men do that, and sometimes we have good conversations while the women listen in. Some of the men just give the standard arguments against Christianity, or try to justify themselves because they know that I know they are not good Muslims. But sometimes they seem to want to know. The younger ones, who are "off the rails" and looked down on by the community, seem to be attracted by Jesus.

'I find I have to be careful not to be side-tracked. We can talk a lot about rituals and law, and it can turn into a kind of religious competition: "I pray more than you do. Our people are more sensible about alcohol than yours." That's not the point, is it? Sometimes, I need to say that being teetotal might not mean that you know God any better. And that is the point, isn't it?

'Since I stopped trying to "witness" all the time, I've been much more relaxed, and I think the women feel that too. It used to be quite a strain visiting them, but now I enjoy it. I feel that we are really friends.

'I love my Asian friends, but I still feel tired after a visit and often get discouraged. I think it's a spiritual thing – I sometimes feel quite oppressed. Prayer for my friends is hard too. I find that I pray a lot before I visit them, but it's mainly because I feel inadequate. I don't pray for them as much as I should.

'What helps most is meeting other Christians who have Asian friends. We can encourage one another and pray together. It's especially good when several Christians know the same Asian families.'

TO THINK ABOUT

- What were the differences between the situations encountered by Bruce and Claire?

- What things within their situations made it difficult for Bruce and Claire to share their faith? What things made it easy?

- What things within Bruce and Claire themselves made it difficult for them to share their faith? What things made it easy?

- Do you think you are more like Bruce or more like Claire?

Opportunities to talk about Jesus happen in many different ways. Jesus himself spoke to people as they asked questions, and often used everyday happenings as his starting point.

The key is to know the Gospels well enough to be able to tell the right story at the right time.

Richard was walking down the road when he saw a man collapsed on the pavement. It was Jason, a notorious alcoholic. Richard helped him into his house and called the doctor. Jason was ill, and his house was in a mess. Richard needed help, so he asked some Muslim boys he knew, who were hanging about in the street, to come and clean Jason's house. 'No way!' they said. 'How could you touch him? How could you go into his house? He's a bad man.' So Richard told them the parable of the Good Samaritan, and they got the point: no human being is untouchable. No place is so unclean that we cannot go there to help a person in need. Together, Richard and the Muslim boys cleaned the flat and looked after Jason until he was better.

TO THINK ABOUT

- Why do you think the boys were shocked at the idea of helping Jason?

- What good news did they learn?

- Think about some of your meetings with Muslim, Hindu or Sikh friends. Were there times when you could have told a Bible story? If you did tell the story, how did your friends react?

Sometimes, you will need to be aware of the ways in which your faith may fulfil your friend's faith:

'Why don't you wash your hands before you read the Bible?' asked Mahmud. 'And why don't you wash before you say your prayers?' 'Well,' I answered, 'I wouldn't read my Bible with my hands dirty, because I wouldn't want to spoil it. But I do make sure I'm clean when I pray. I don't do it by washing my hands, though. I do it by praying in the Name of Jesus. The most important thing is to be clean inside – to be forgiven for all my wrong thoughts and all the things I have done wrong. We believe that Jesus does that.'

TO THINK ABOUT
- Think about other religious practices – ritual prayers, food laws, festivals. How could you explain why you don't do things the same way as your Asian friend? How could you use them to point to Jesus?

On many occasions, you can offer to pray for your friend. Sometimes the Lord will answer in unexpected ways.

Rashik was a collaborator in an armed affray that took place in his own street. His Christian friend witnessed the incident and the situation leading up to it. He wanted to help the police, provided they were willing to take account of the circumstances which, he thought, made Rashik's actions understandable. The police were interested only in the actual incident.

Rashik asked his friend to be a witness. 'I will have to tell the truth, that you were involved,' he replied. Rashik agreed. 'I have prayed to Jesus, and I believe that this will not go any further,' said the friend. He gave his account to the police, and the result was that Rashik was cautioned and told to keep out of trouble for the next three years.

TO THINK ABOUT
- Telling Bible stories, seeing where your friend's faith points to Jesus, praying for your friend – when have you had opportunities to share your faith in these ways?

- How has your friend shared his or her faith with you?

- How has God been answering your prayers for your friend?

Sometimes, you can take the initiative. Many Muslims, Hindus and Sikhs will be delighted to have a well-presented portion of scripture at Christmas or Easter. Beautiful calendars and posters with Bible verses in Asian languages and in English are also acceptable gifts. There are many resources available.

I've been visiting Surinder for the past four years, as a volunteer English teacher. She's got a job now, although I don't think that's anything to do with me. Her English is a bit better though. I'm getting a bit fed up. I'm not sure we're getting anywhere.

Sharing faith? Well, we have had some talk about it. She doesn't seem to know what she's supposed to believe, so that makes discussion difficult. Yes, I could give her the Jesus video – she watches lots of videos, and I think she might like that. She could try it in English, to practise her language; but she might also like it in Punjabi. She'd be surprised to hear it in her own language. She doesn't really believe that Punjabis can be Christians.

I had been praying for the corner shopkeeper for a year, but I didn't know how to speak to him about Christ. I just used to drop in every few days, buy a newspaper, and talk about everyday things. Then someone gave me a copy of Ye Sach Hai. It's a paper full of stories about Asians who have come to Christ. I gave it to him. He read it, and was interested. 'I didn't know there were Asian Christians in Britain,' he said. 'I'd like to meet some.' We have just one Indian family at our local church, so I've invited him to the Christmas carol service. He's really pleased. 'I've never been into a church before,' he says. 'I've always wondered what it would be like.' Maybe after Christmas I can give him a gospel.

IDEAS
• Find out if your local Christian bookshop keeps literature, tapes, videos, calendars and posters which may

be suitable for your Asian friends. If not, why not tell them about the resource centres listed at the end of this book?

• If your church has any outreach into the local community, discuss with the leaders how you could let Asian neighbours know you are interested in them, too.

You could also introduce your friend to other Christian people. After all, you are not operating on your own. As Claire needed the fellowship and prayer support of other Christians, so do you. Especially helpful can be fellowship with Christians from other cultures, including those from Muslim, Sikh or Hindu families. Together, you can learn to understand one another, cross cultural barriers and see how different people respond to Jesus.

Sharing the gospel is not just our job or your job: it is the job of the whole Body of Christ. Your Asian friends will need to see that you are part of a family, a community and a worldwide fellowship, from 'every tribe and language and people and nation' (Revelation 5:9) into which they, too, can be welcomed. They also need to see how Christians relate with each other, for that, says the Bible, is how people will recognise Christ:

> By this all men will know that you are my disciples, if you love one another. *(John 13:35)*

> No one has ever seen God, but if we love one another, God lives in us and his love is made complete in us. *(1 John 4:12)*

As you become part of your friend's family, you can invite them to be part of yours – of your Christian family as well as your blood family. The greatest witnesses to Christ are Christians who give true friendship to each other.

To think about

- When the Hindus, Sikhs and Muslims you know look at the church, what do they see?

- How can you help your friend to see Christians loving each other?

People do come to Christ

Christine had been my friend for years. She had often tried to talk about Jesus, but frankly I wasn't interested. I may not have been a very religious Muslim, but I knew (or so I thought) that Christianity was not the Right Way. Then I went through a difficult time. My mother was very ill, my sister's marriage broke up, and I had problems at work. Christine was away at the time, but she started sending me these beautiful verses. I found them so comforting. When she came back, I asked her where she found them. Did she write them herself, or what? 'They're from the Psalms,' she said. 'You know – in the Bible.' I was shocked. I'd been told I would be cursed if I read the Bible, and here I was, being blessed by it.

That was just the beginning. I asked for a Bible, and have never looked back. Following Jesus is just the best thing that's happened to me. My mother doesn't like it much, but she's pleased because I'm happy, and she lets me stay at home no matter what other people say – and they say a lot! Some of our community won't speak to her any more, but 'You are still my daughter,' she says. 'Nothing can change that.' She didn't even seem to mind too much when I got baptised, though my father (they're divorced, so he doesn't live with us) says he never wants to see me again.

Not everyone who comes to Christ is as fortunate as Christine's friend. Some find that their families are embarrassed about their new faith. Some are thrown out of their homes. Some even get death threats. If your friend comes to

Christ, your friendship will be even more important than before. He or she will need to feel part of your family as well as part of the family of the church.

When Sitender, a Sikh girl in her early twenties, announced that she had become a Christian, she was thrown out of the house. She went to live in a different town. About a year later, her father died. She very much wanted to go to the funeral, but was threatened with violence should she dare to show her face. She now has no contact with her mother or the rest of her family.

To THINK ABOUT
• What might be the needs of a white English girl estranged from her family?

• How might Sitender's needs be different?

Welcoming someone from a different culture into our church family can change the way we do things.

Mrs Manek gave her life to the Lord at the age of 62. She was already separated from her Hindu husband, and her children had little to do with her. They had their own families to look after. Her new family was the church. They recognised her need for regular visitors, and drew up a visiting rota. However, when Mrs Manek was asked whether anyone had visited her, she would say 'No' even though someone had been to her on that very morning. The church asked an Asian Christian for help. She spent some time with Mrs Manek. Mrs Manek confided that she did get people dropping in regularly, mainly on their way home from the market. They would sit with her for 15–20 minutes, have a cup of tea, and leave. In Mrs Manek's culture, the first half hour of a visit scarcely gets past, 'How are you?' It would take at least an hour before she would feel free to share any deep needs. She felt that church members were just using her as a tea stop.

The church members began to accept Mrs Manek's needs, and make longer visits. They were also able to help Mrs Manek understand their needs, and she was happy to see those who came just for a cup of tea.

IDEA
Invite your church leadership group to read these two stories. Ask them how the church can be prepared to welcome your friend when he or she comes to Christ.

Even if they don't come to Christ...
'If I don't become a Christian, will you still be my friend?'

This book has been more about friendship than about evangelism. This is because we don't think of friendship as a means to evangelism, but as an expression of Christ's love through his people. He is the friend of sinners. He is the one we can always trust. He is the one who invites us in and who is willing to eat with us. He is the one who continues to love us even when we reject him.

This is why friendship is often the way in which people can hear of Christ and come to him. The friendship of God towards us *is* the gospel. As we model his friendship, people will come to know him.

God is the one who:

– knows us as we are;

– understands where we have been;

– accepts who we have become;

– and still gently invites us to grow.

• He *knows* just what is in your friend's heart. He knows how much of the gospel your friend understands, how much response she has made, and why she does not want to become a Christian. He also knows just what your friend needs.

75

- He *understands* your friend's upbringing and family, and all the pressures he may be under. He understands where she hurts, why she is afraid and what benefits her faith may be giving her. He sees where she has been, and is prepared to watch over the rest of her journey through life.

- He *accepts* us. Perhaps you find this one difficult. Does God really accept who we have become? Does he not want to change us? Yes, he does, and sometimes he disciplines us severely. But he knows who we are and does not demand that we change before he loves us. In fact, he knows that we cannot change without his love and his grace and his power. He works with what we are, not with what we ought to be. So he accepts your friend for who she is, and patiently waits for her response to his love.

- He *invites* us. Although he accepts us for what we are, God gives us hope that we don't have to stay as we are. We can change and grow into the people he made us to be. He does not force us but, rather, he invites us. He is offering your friend the opportunity to grow in understanding and to come to him.

Friend, good friend, one of the family

Jesus told his disciples, 'You are my friends' (John 15:14). We can think of him introducing us to his Father: 'This is Shaylesh: he is one of us. This is Ida: she is part of our family.'

Let us therefore introduce Jesus to our Hindu and Sikh and Muslim friends: he is one of us, part of our family. We have welcomed him to eat with us: our friendship with God is bonded. We can celebrate the end of all our disputes with him. And we can call others to 'share salt' with him and with us in the great extended family of the worldwide, multi-cultural church.

FOR FURTHER HELP

Two stories giving insights into culture and faith

- Ram Gidoomal with Mike Fearon, *Sari and Chips*, Monarch, 1993: a Hindu comes to Britain from East Africa; this story describes how he adjusts to a new culture and comes to Christ.

- Narindar Mehat with Margaret Wardell, *When Love Prevails*, OM, 1998: in her village in India, a Sikh girl seeks God; when she comes to Britain to be married, she eventually finds him in Christ.

A handbook for Christian women relating to Muslim women

- Sally Sutcliffe, *Aishah, my Sister*, Paternoster, 1998: a wealth of information, stories, theology and practical advice from Christian women living and working amongst Muslims in Britain.

Resources mentioned in Sharing the Salt

- The *Jesus* video is available in the main Asian languages of Britain; contact the Faith to Faith Resource Centre (see below).

- Ye Sach Hai: contact PO Box 597, Dagenham, Essex, RM8 2PP; an occasional colour broadsheet aimed at encouraging British Asians to consider the gospel; includes testimonies from people from Muslim, Sikh, Hindu and Christian families, who have come to know Jesus.

• The story of Ruth is retold in Testament (The Bible in Animation), available on video from the Bible Society, Stonehill Green, Westlea, Swindon, SN5 7DG.

Resource Centres

• Asian Books, PO Box 43, Sutton, Surrey, SM2 5WL; tel (0181) 395 8281. Scripture and books, in Asian languages and English.

• Faith to Faith Resource Centre, 10 Church Lane, Oldham, Greater Manchester, OL1 3AN. Books, audio tapes and videos, in Asian languages and English.

• Kitab Book Services, PO Box 16, Failsworth, Manchester, M35 9QL; tel (0161) 678 6838; email kitab.uk@domini.org. Books, Bibles and cards; videos in Asian, Oriental and Eastern European languages; books in English, particularly on Islam.

Courses, consultancy, people who can help you

• Alliance of Asian Christians, Carrs Lane Church Centre, Carrs Lane, Birmingham, B4 7SX; tel (0121) 633 4533. Encourages the development of the Asian Christian community, and builds bridges between Asian Christians and denominational churches; can put you in touch with your nearest Asian Christian fellowship.

• Asian Equip, 297 Haslucks Road, Shirley, Solihull, B90 2LW; tel (0121) 744 3057; email east+west@bigfoot.com. Provides training material on video along with many other resources; organises day conferences in the Birmingham area.

- Evangelical Alliance Other Faiths Forum, Whitefield House, 186 Kennington Park Road, London, SE11 4BT; tel (0171) 207 2100. Networks agencies working with people of other faiths in Britain; occasional conferences and publications.

- Faith to Faith, Trinity College, Stoke Hill, Bristol, BS9 1JP; tel (0117) 968 2803; email faith@trinity-bris.ac.uk. A team of consultants offering advice and teaching on mission and ministry amongst people of other faiths anywhere in Britain; runs 'Cross and Crescent' courses on Islam.

- Ministry amongst Asians in Britain, Cornerstone House, 5 Ethel Street, Birmingham, B2 4BG; tel (0121) 642 7771; email davidcorfe@mabham.globalnet.co.uk. A team of people with experience and skills in cross-cultural mission; operates in twenty different locations in Britain.

Other titles in the 'Relating Good News' series
- *Wake up to Work: Friendship and Faith in the Workplace*, Geoff Shattock.

- *Man to Man: Friendship and Faith*, Steven Croft.

- *Friendship Matters*, David Spriggs and Darrell Jackson.